THE EARNHARDT NASCAR DYNASTY

THE LEGACY OF DALE SR. AND DALE JR.

Stephanie Watson

New York

To my husband, who makes my heart race every day

Published in 2010 by The Rosen Publishing Group, Inc.
29 East 21st Street, New York, NY 10010

"NASCAR" is a registered trademark of the National Association for Stock Car Auto Racing, Inc.

Library of Congress Cataloging-in-Publication Data

Watson, Stephanie, 1969–
The Earnhardt NASCAR dynasty: the legacy of Dale Sr. and Dale Jr. / Stephanie Watson.—1st ed.
      p. cm.—(Sports families)
Includes bibliographical references and index.
ISBN 978-1-4358-3551-1 (library binding)
ISBN 978-1-4358-8512-7 (pbk)
ISBN 978-1-4358-8513-4 (6 pack)
1. Earnhardt, Dale, 1951–2001. 2. Earnhardt, Dale, Jr. 3. Stock car drivers—United States—Biography. 4. Stock car racing—United States. I. Title.
GV1032.A1W37 2010
796.72092—dc22
[B]
                                                                        2009025860

Manufactured in the United States of America

CPSIA Compliance Information: Batch #LW10YA: For Further Information contact Rosen Publishing, New York, New York at 1-800-237-9932

On the cover: Dale Earnhardt Sr. hugs his son Dale Jr. after Dale Sr. won the International Race of Champions at the Daytona International Speedway on February 18, 2000. Dale Jr. finished fifth.

Contents

Dale Earnhardt Sr. is at the head of the pack during the February 18, 2001, Daytona 500. This Daytona 500 was his last race.

It was February 18, 2001. The 43rd annual Daytona 500 was ready to start at Daytona International Speedway at Daytona Beach, Florida. For fans of the National Association for Stock Car Auto Racing (NASCAR), this was the biggest race of the year, as big as the Super Bowl is to football fans. The stands were packed with some 170,000 fans, many of whom had camped out in the infield for several days leading up to the race.

Forty-three drivers were told to start their engines. The flag was waved, and the racers took off around the 2.5-mile (4 kilometer) track, reaching speeds of more than 175 miles per hour (281 km per hour).

The drivers in this race were the best in NASCAR. Still, they had good reason to worry. When any driver saw a black Chevy Monte Carlo with the white #3 on its side in his rearview mirror, he knew "The Intimidator" was on his tail. He was either going to get passed or bumped from behind.

"The Intimidator" was the nickname given to legendary NASCAR racer Dale Earnhardt Sr. for his bold and aggressive racing style. That style had served him well. He had won NASCAR's top series, the Winston Cup (called the Sprint Cup Series since 2008), seven times. He had won 76 Winston Cup races in all and had finished in the top five in 281 races. He was tied with Richard Petty for the most Winston Cup championships in circuit history. Dale Sr. had become so popular in NASCAR that H. A. (Humpy) Wheeler, president of Lowe's Motor Speedway in Charlotte, North Carolina, had called him the "Michael Jordan of our sport."

Dale Sr. had earned the title in his own right, but he had inherited his toughness on the track from his father, Ralph Earnhardt. Ralph was one of stock car racing's earliest stars. He had won NASCAR's Late Model Sportsman championship in the 1950s, and NASCAR later named him one of its top 50 drivers.

The only time father and son had driven together was at Metrolina Speedway outside of Charlotte in the early 1970s. With just a few laps to go, Dale Sr. was in fourth place, but he couldn't get past the driver in front of him. Ralph came up from behind and his car made contact with Dale Sr.'s car, pushing him right past the other driver. Yet he didn't let his son win. Ralph won the race, and Dale Sr. finished third.

Dale Sr. became such a fierce competitor that a few times when he had raced his own son, Dale Jr., he had bumped him out of his way. But at this Daytona 500, the elder Earnhardt was playing the role of protector instead of competitor.

With just five laps to go in the 500-lap race, Dale Earnhardt Sr. had moved into third position. In first place was Michael Waltrip, a member of his racing team. In second place was Dale Earnhardt Jr.

Dale Sr. used his car to block the other drivers behind him. Meanwhile, he talked to Michael and Dale Jr. on the radio, instructing them where to drive to stay in front. As he helped Michael and Dale Jr. move closer to the finish line, his car was suddenly bumped by Sterling Martin's car. The #3 Monte Carlo veered left. Then it quickly turned right and was hit by an oncoming car. On the final section of the final lap in the Daytona 500, Dale Sr.'s car smashed straight into the wall at 180 miles per hour (290 km per hour).

From the outside, the crash didn't look so bad. Dale Sr. had been in far worse-looking wrecks. (In 1976, his car flipped five times at Atlanta International Speedway, and he walked away with just a cut on his hand.) Yet race fans know that the worse a crash looks, the less dangerous it really is. Earlier in the Daytona 500, 19 cars had smashed into one another in a really ugly accident. Tony Stewart's car had flown into the air, tearing the hood off of Bobby Labonte's car as it flipped. Yet all of the drivers walked

Michael Waltrip (#15) speeds across the finish line first at the Daytona 500, with Dale Jr. (#8) directly behind him.

away without major injuries. When a car flips and falls apart, it absorbs the impact of a crash. When a car stays intact, the driver absorbs the impact. Dale Sr.'s car was almost completely intact.

Michael Waltrip sped across the finish line with Dale Jr. close behind him. Meanwhile, there was no movement from Dale Sr.'s car.

LOSS OF A LEGEND

At 7:00 PM that evening, NASCAR president Mike Helton delivered the sad news on television. "This is undoubtedly one of the toughest announcements I have ever personally had to make," he said. "We've lost Dale Earnhardt." The Intimidator was gone. He was only 49 years old.

There have been many families in the history of stock car racing: Lee, Richard, Kyle, and Adam Petty. Darrell and Michael Waltrip. Buck and Buddy Baker. Clifford and Davey Allison. Yet the Earnhardts are among the greatest racing families. Ralph, Dale Sr., Dale Jr., and two of Dale Sr.'s other children, Kerry and Kelley, have all been part of the sport. Dale Sr. was considered one of NASCAR's most popular drivers. Losing him hit fans hard.

After Dale Sr.'s death, fans drove across the country to visit Dale Earnhardt, Inc. (DEI), his company in Mooresville, North Carolina. They made makeshift memorials of flowers, cards, and racing memorabilia at the racetracks where he had driven. They remembered his legacy. Grown men cried. One man in Florida plowed a #3 measuring 353 feet (100 meters) in his pasture to honor Dale. A 59-year-old fan named Becky Duckworth told *People* magazine in March 2001, "Besides my husband, Dale Earnhardt is the only man I've ever loved."

Dale Earnhardt Sr. died doing what he loved most. "Earnhardt is the only one I know who if NASCAR was to call and say, 'Guys, we've got an empty grandstand this week, there's no money, and we need all of you to pay $5,000 to enter the race,' he'd be the only car that would show up," driver Bobby Hamilton told *Sports Illustrated* in February 2001. Driver Johnny Benson said in the same issue, "NASCAR lost its greatest driver and probably the greatest driver it will ever have."

Chapter One

THE INTIMIDATOR

The man who would one day be known as the Intimidator was born on April 29, 1951, in Kannapolis, a small city about 20 miles (32.2 km) northeast of Charlotte, North Carolina. Kannapolis used to be a mill town. Just about everyone who lived in the city worked in the textile mills, including Dale Sr.'s father, Ralph. His mother, Martha, worked at a diner near the mills.

It's fitting that Dale Earnhardt Sr., a future car racing legend, grew up in an area of the city known as "Car Town." The streets were all named after car models, such as Buick, Hudson, and DeSoto. The Earnhardts lived at 1412 Sedan Avenue.

North Carolina was also the birthplace of stock car racing. The first Strictly Stock race (the equivalent of today's Sprint Cup) was held at the Charlotte Speedway in 1949. Ralph Earnhardt was one of the first NASCAR drivers. In his #8 car (his grandson Dale Jr. would later make the same number famous on his own car), Ralph won the Late Model Sportsman championship in 1956.

The sport of NASCAR racing in the 1950s was very different from what it is today, though. Back then, drivers could barely earn enough money to support their families. Even though Ralph won 350 races during his career, he usually didn't earn more than $150 to $200 a race. He had to continue working in the mills to make enough money to support his wife and children.

Ralph Earnhardt (#75) tries to pass another driver on the first turn of the Rebel 300 at Darlington, South Carolina, on May 14, 1962. Competitors considered Ralph an innovator and tough race driver.

Of the five Earnhardt children, Dale Sr. was the one who was the most entranced by racing. When he was just a boy, Dale Sr. used to watch his father race on the dirt tracks in Monroe and Hickory, North Carolina, and Columbia and Greenville, South Carolina. Dale Sr. also watched his father build cars in the cinderblock garage that Ralph had constructed behind the house. Eventually, he was old enough to help out in the garage. By the time he was a teenager, he had joined his father's racing pit crew, along with his brothers, Randy and Denny.

When he was just 16, Dale Sr. quit school. His father was very unhappy about it, but Dale Sr. wanted to be a race car driver, and nothing was going to stop him.

THE STRUGGLE TO RACE

At just 17 years old, Dale Sr. married Latane Brown. They had a son, Kerry. To support his new family, Dale Sr. worked various odd jobs that included being a mechanic and a welder. But all he really wanted to do was race. By the time Dale Sr. was 19, his first marriage was over, but his racing career was just starting.

In 1970, Dale Sr. drove his first race on a dirt track. His first race car was a 1956 Ford Club sedan. There was a mistake when the paint for the car was mixed and it turned out pink. Even while driving a pink car, Dale Sr. proved himself

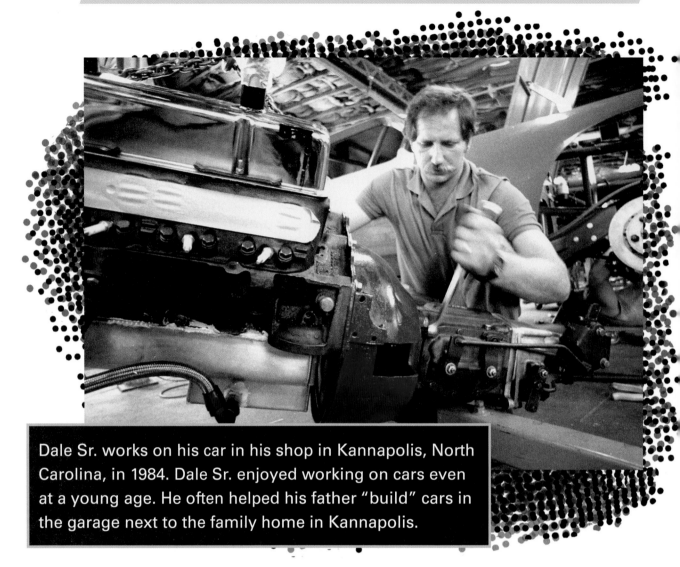

Dale Sr. works on his car in his shop in Kannapolis, North Carolina, in 1984. Dale Sr. enjoyed working on cars even at a young age. He often helped his father "build" cars in the garage next to the family home in Kannapolis.

to be a tough competitor on the track. "You could see that Dale knew what he was doing," said the owner of that Ford, David Oliver, as quoted in the Leigh Montville book *At the Altar of Speed*. "He knew when to make the move and when not to make the move, where the holes were."

Dale Sr. was adept on the track, but he knew that he needed a better car if he was going to win races. He asked race car owner James Miller if he could drive one of his Ford Falcons. Miller said he could drive one—but only if he fixed it up first. Dale Sr. worked on that car for two nights straight to earn the right to race it.

THE INTIMIDATOR'S QUIET SIDE

Dale Earnhardt Sr. may have been intimidating on the racetrack, but at home he had a much gentler side. Friends and family members remember his huge smile, warm laugh, and great sense of humor. He loved the outdoors and nature. His favorite spot was the family's 300-acre (121 hectares) North Carolina farm. He enjoyed the solitude that he found there. "Sometimes, I walk all over the place by myself, and other times I walk out into the woods and sit down with my back against a tree and listen to tree frogs, katydids, bluebirds, and I watch other forms of wildlife," he told *American Forests* magazine in 2004.

After driving Miller's car for a while, Dale Sr. joined the Russell Brothers racing team. In his first year with the Russell Brothers, he won 17 times. Like his father, Dale Sr. raced on dirt tracks, most of them in North Carolina and South Carolina. His first win was at Concord Speedway in Midland, North Carolina.

In 1971, Dale Sr. married Brenda Gee. They had two children. Daughter Kelley was born on August 28, 1972. Dale Jr. was born on October 10, 1974. Dale Sr. was racing more often and getting better at the sport, but his winnings still didn't pay the bills. The family lived in a double-wide trailer behind the house where he grew up on Sedan Avenue. Dale Sr. worked odd jobs to make ends meet.

In 1973, when Dale Sr. was just 22 years old, he lost his hero and mentor. Ralph Earnhardt died of a heart attack while working on his car. He was just 45 years old. Dale Sr. often said that his father was the biggest influence on his life. Though he missed his father terribly, Dale Sr. knew that he needed to keep going if he wanted to achieve his dream of becoming a successful race car driver.

On May 25, 1975, Dale Sr. makes his NASCAR Cup debut in the World 600 at Charlotte Motor Speedway (now called Lowe's Motor Speedway) in North Carolina. In that race, he drove a Dodge (#8) owned by Ed Negre, and started 33rd and finished 22nd.

DALE SR.'S WINSTON CUP DEBUT

In 1974, Dale Sr. switched from dirt to asphalt (pavement) racing and joined the Sportsman division of NASCAR (later named the Busch Series; now it's called the NASCAR Nationwide Series). This series is the equivalent of the minor leagues in baseball. It's where drivers get their start on their way to the big leagues—the Winston Cup (today called the Sprint Cup) Series.

On May 25, 1975, Dale Sr. made his stock car racing debut in the World 600 at Lowe's Motor Speedway in Charlotte. He finished 22nd and won more than $1,900. It was a lot of money at the time. Over the next three years, Dale Sr. drove in a few more Cup races, but he could never win. The problem was, he still didn't have a good enough car.

Then he met California businessman Rod Osterlund. Osterlund wanted to put together his own NASCAR team, and he had a lot of money to make it happen. He hired the best mechanics and bought the best cars. He chose Dale Earnhardt Sr. as his driver.

In 1978, Dale Sr. got his start driving for Osterlund at the Dixie 500 in Atlanta, Georgia. Finally behind the wheel of a decent car, he was able to finish in fourth place. Within a year, he went from being an unknown to being one of the most exciting new drivers in NASCAR.

LITTLE "E"

While Dale Sr. was starting to make a name for himself on the NASCAR circuit, his son was growing up in Concord, North Carolina. By the time Dale Jr. was three years old, his parents had divorced. At first, he and his sister, Kelley, lived with their mother, Brenda. Then the family's house burned down, and they went to live with their father.

All of Dale Sr.'s children—Kerry, Kelley, and Dale Jr.—fell in love with the sport of racing. (Dale Sr., Kerry, and Dale Jr. would compete against one another just once, in a 2000 Winston Cup race at Michigan Speedway.) Although Dale Sr.'s career was heating up and he was often away from

The Earnhardts pose for this family photo in 1987. From left to right are Kelley, Dale Sr., Dale Jr., and Teresa.

home at races, he would sometimes take Dale Jr. to the track with him during the summers.

Dale Jr. started driving go-karts when he was 12, but after he was thrown off the go-kart a few times, his father banned him from the activity. He would have to wait to race until he was older and had his driver's license.

That moment came in 1989, when Dale Jr. was 17 years old. He and his half-brother, Kerry, chipped in $200 to buy an old Chevrolet Monte Carlo. They fixed up the car and were ready to race, but Dale Sr. stopped the project. He wouldn't let his son race until he had driven the car through at least 150 practice laps. One day, Dale Jr. drove those 150 laps without stopping.

"Well, you didn't hit anything. Let's see how you do in traffic," Dale Sr. replied, according to Jeff Savage in his book, *Dale Earnhardt, Jr.*

He and Kerry took turns racing their Monte Carlo on local short tracks. Dale Jr. didn't win any races, but he did learn a lot about the sport.

RACING FAMILY

While Dale Jr. was learning, his dad put him to work on his older sister Kelley's pit crew. Kelley was also a talented driver. However, it was hard being a woman in NASCAR, where there were so few female drivers. (Kelley eventually got out of racing and went to work for Dale Jr.'s company.)

Soon, Dale Jr. and Kerry started their own racing team. They traveled to Myrtle Beach, South Carolina, and other tracks in the South to race. Still, Dale Jr. didn't think his career would be in race car driving. He thought he might become a mechanic instead. He was working part-time at his father's car dealership, Dale Earnhardt Chevrolet, and he was very good at repairing cars. He saw himself moving up through the ranks in the dealership's service department. Life was about to take a very big turn for Dale Jr.

Chapter Two

A NASCAR LEGEND

Driving Rod Osterlund's #2 car, Dale Earnhardt Sr. started to move up in the racing ranks. Finally, in 1979, he earned his first victory at Bristol Motor Speedway in Tennessee. He also won the Atlanta 500 that year. Dale Sr. finished out the year with the seventh highest number of points. (Drivers are awarded points depending on how high they finish in a race.) He won about $237,575. For being the best newcomer in his sport, Dale Sr. was named NASCAR's Rookie of the Year.

The next year, 1980, was another good year for Dale Sr. He won his first Winston Cup championship, and he had the highest number of points among all the drivers for nearly the entire season.

Dale Earnhardt Sr. was becoming famous—and rich. But he was still crashing and having constant trouble with his cars. In one race, his ignition cut out. In another, his engine failed. During the 1981 season, he didn't win a single race. Then his sponsor, Rod Osterlund, decided to get out of the racing business. Dale Sr. was on his own, without a team.

BEGINNING OF AN EMPIRE

Everything changed for Dale Sr. in 1983, when he teamed up with fellow NASCAR driver Richard Childress to form Richard Childress Racing. Childress insisted that the team build their own cars from the ground up. For the first time, Dale Sr. was driving cars that were as tough as he was.

Dale Earnhardt Sr. celebrates his first Winston Cup win on April 1, 1979, at the Bristol Motor Speedway in Bristol, Tennessee. He drove Rod Osterlund's car in the race.

By the mid-1980s, Dale Sr. was driving the best cars in the circuit. He was also becoming legendary for his ability on the track. "Nobody drove the way he did. Nobody did the things he did," said his racing rival, Darrell Waltrip, as quoted in *At the Altar of Speed*.

Things were also starting to come together in Dale Sr.'s personal life. After two failed marriages, he met Teresa Houston. She was the niece of Sportsman driver Tommy Houston. After Dale Sr. broke his leg during a crash at Pocono International Raceway, he proposed to Teresa from his hospital bed. She said yes, and they were married on November 14, 1982. In 1988, they had a daughter, who they named Taylor Nicole.

Back on the track, Richard Childress Racing dominated NASCAR in the mid-1980s. Dale Sr. won five races in 1985 and was the Winston Cup champion. The following year, he won five races and his second Winston Cup championship (with Richard Childress Racing). In 1987, he won 11 times, including a third Winston Cup championship. That was also the year that Dale Sr. made one of the most famous racing moves in NASCAR history.

THE PASS IN THE GRASS

Dale Earnhardt Sr. was having an incredible 1987 season. He had won six out his first eight races. In May of that year, he drove in a three-part series called the All-Star Race at Charlotte Motor Speedway. The prize was $200,000. The final race, called the Shootout, was only 10 laps long. Dale Sr. was determined to win.

Going into the race, Bill Elliott was in the lead. He had already won the first two races that day. Dale Sr. wasn't about to let him win the third. In the first lap, Elliott and Geoff Bodine bumped into each other and spun out. Dale Sr. grabbed the lead.

Bill was convinced that Dale Sr. had caused him to make contact with Geoff's car. He took off after Dale Sr. When he caught up with him, he gave

Dale Sr. gets ready for the NASCAR Sovran Bank 500 (today a Nextel Cup event) race in 1987. He led the race in 156 of the 500 laps and won.

the #3 car a bump. Dale Sr. bumped him back. They went back and forth, hitting each other like bumper cars as they sped around the track.

At the fourth turn, Elliott bumped Dale Sr. again and sent him careening off the track. Dale Sr. ended up on the strip of grass that separates the track from the pit road. It's almost impossible to keep a race car under control on grass, especially a car that is going 150 miles per hour (241 km per hour). Dale Sr. not only kept his car going forward, but he also hit the accelerator. He sped back onto the racetrack ahead of Bill Elliott and won the race.

DALE SR.'S CAREER STATS

The following are some of the highlights from Dale Earnhardt Sr.'s NASCAR career:

1979 One win, 11 top 5 finishes, $237,575 in winnings
1980 Five wins, 19 top 5 finishes, $451,360 in winnings
1983 Two wins, 9 top 5 finishes, $396,991 in winnings
1984 Two wins, 12 top 5 finishes, second at Daytona 500, $509,805 in winnings
1985 Four wins, 10 top 5 finishes, $457,658 in winnings
1986 Five wins, 16 top 5 finishes, $868,100 in winnings
1987 Eleven wins, 21 top 5 finishes, $1,041,120 in winnings
1990 Nine wins, 18 top 5 finishes, $1,307,830 in winnings
1993 Six wins, 17 top 5 finishes, second at Daytona 500, $1,326,240 in winnings
1994 Four wins, 20 top 5 finishes, $1,465,890 in winnings
1998 One win, 5 top 5 finishes, won the Daytona 500, $2,611,100 in winnings
1999 Three wins, 7 top 5 finishes, $2,712,089 in winnings
2000 Two wins, 13 top 5 finishes, $3,701,390 in winnings

(Source: NASCAR.com)

Dale Sr.'s maneuver became known as the "Pass in the Grass." Many people consider it the greatest move in the history of car racing.

THE MICHAEL JORDAN OF RACING

Dale Sr. made many other great maneuvers on the track, bumping a lot of drivers out of his way to get to the finish line. He just kept on winning. In

Dale Sr. signs autographs before a race in Martinsville, Virginia. Although some disliked his aggressive racing style, most adored the Intimidator. Many say he might be the greatest driver of all time.

1990, he won nine races and took his fourth Winston Cup championship. He earned more than $3 million that year, which was a record for a driver at the time. By 1994, Dale Sr. had won his seventh Winston Cup title and was tied with race car legend Richard Petty for the most Winston Cup wins.

Even people who weren't NASCAR fans started to take notice of Dale Earnhardt Sr. In 1997, he became the first race car driver to appear on a box of Wheaties cereal. Fans wore T-shirts and hats emblazoned with the #3. They painted the #3 logo on their cars.

By 2000, a quarter of NASCAR's entire $1.1 billion merchandising sales were for Dale Earnhardt Sr. products, according to Bill Hewitt in *People* magazine. Dale Sr. owned trucks, all-terrain vehicles (ATVs), his own corporate jet and helicopter, and a Hatteras yacht, which was 76 feet (23 m) in length. *Forbes* magazine put him at #40 on its list of the "100 Richest Celebrities," between Rosie O'Donnell and the rock band Kiss. Dale Sr. had become the Michael Jordan of racing.

THE DAYTONA 500

By the late 1990s, Dale Sr. was considered the best in his sport. He had won seven NASCAR Cup Series championships. Yet he still had not won the coveted Daytona 500, the equivalent to the World Series or Super Bowl in racing. He had run the Daytona 500 19 times and finished second three times, but that top spot kept eluding him.

Some people thought Dale Sr.'s losing streak was a curse. He kept having bad luck on the last few laps of the Daytona 500 race. In 1985, his engine failed. The next year, he ran out of gas with only three laps to go.

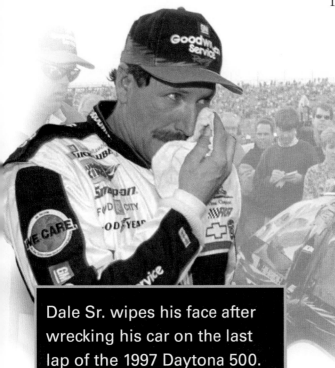

In 1997, Dale Sr. still didn't win, but he had one of his most memorable Daytona 500 finishes. On the last lap, he was in second place, fighting with Jeff Gordon for the lead, when his car made contact with Jeff's car. Dale Sr. lost control of his car. It smashed into

Dale Sr. wipes his face after wrecking his car on the last lap of the 1997 Daytona 500. It was his 19th attempt to win.

the wall at close to 200 miles per hour (322 km per hour) and then flipped several times before landing in the infield. Dale Sr. crawled out of his mangled car and was walking to the ambulance when he looked back and thought, "Man, the wheels ain't knocked off that car yet," according to *At the Altar of Speed*. In true Dale Earnhardt Sr. fashion, he got back into his Monte Carlo and finished the race in 31st place.

The following year was one of Dale Sr.'s worst seasons ever. He was winless for the first time since 1981. As he attempted his 20th Daytona 500, people wondered if the 47-year-old could ever win it. But Dale Sr. was determined. Before the race, he met a six-year-old girl named Wessa Miller, who was in a wheelchair. Wessa gave Dale Sr. her lucky penny, telling him it would help him win the race.

No one can know for sure if the penny really gave him good luck, but Dale Sr. was able to hold on to the lead for most of the 200-lap race. When he crossed the finish line in first place, the crowd of 175,000 people stood up and cheered. All the other drivers and their crews stood in a row along the pit road to congratulate him. His eyes teared up. Winning the Daytona 500 had been Dale Sr.'s dream, and he had finally achieved it.

Chapter Three

FOLLOWING IN HIS FATHER'S FOOTSTEPS

After his Daytona 500 victory, Dale Earnhardt Sr. was at the top of his game. He was on a winning streak with Richard Childress Racing. He also had his own racing team, Dale Earnhardt, Inc. (DEI).

By the mid-1990s, Dale Sr. started to notice that his son also had a real knack for race car driving. For someone who was new to the Busch Series, Dale Jr. was making a strong start. In 1996, he finished only one lap behind the winner in a race at Myrtle Beach, South Carolina. It was a big accomplishment for the 22-year-old.

In 1998, Dale Sr. invited his son to join the DEI team. It was one of the best teams in NASCAR, and there was a lot of pressure on Dale Jr. to perform well. It may have been that pressure that caused Dale Jr. to wipe out in his very first Busch Series race with DEI. His car flipped while traveling 170 miles per hour (273 km per hour). Like his father, Dale Jr. wasn't frightened by a terrifying-looking crash. "As I flipped, all I could see was earth, sky, earth, sky, earth, sky," he recalled in his autobiography, *Driver #8*. "Only after the car came to a stop did I realize I had landed upside down."

Despite the crash during his first race with DEI, 1998 turned out to be a good year for Dale Jr. After losing his first few Busch Series races, he finally won the Coca-Cola 300 at Texas Motor Speedway. He went on to win six other races that year and became the Busch Series champion. It was the first time in history that a grandfather, father, and son had all won the NASCAR title.

Dale Jr. gets a hug from his father after winning the Winston All-Star race at Lowe's Motor Speedway in Concord, North Carolina, on May 20, 2000.

FATHER AND SON

In 1999, Dale Jr. raced against his dad in the third round of the International Race of Champions (IROC) at Michigan Speedway. It turned out that Dale Jr. was just as fierce a competitor as his father. In the few times over the years that they raced together, it didn't matter that they were father and son. They were both out to win. In this Michigan race, Dale Sr. and his son

Trivia About Dale Jr.

Who is Dale Earnhardt Jr.? The following are a few facts about the youngest member of the Earnhardt racing dynasty:

His nicknames are "Little E" and "Junior."

He is a big fan of Elvis Presley and Merle Haggard.

He loves taking computers apart and putting them back together again, and playing computer games.

For good luck, he kept a volleyball named "Wilson" in his car during several races.

He's a good cook, and he loves making cheeseburgers.

He collects movie posters.

drove into the final lap running first and second. When Dale Jr. tried to pass his father, Dale Sr. blocked him and the two cars smacked into one another. Dale Sr. ended up winning the race by 7,000ths of a second, but father and son couldn't agree on who had caused the collision. Though they were competitors, the two men had great love and admiration for each other.

In 2000, Dale Jr. moved up into the big leagues of racing: the Winston Cup Series. He finally got the chance to drive in his first Daytona 500 in February. Just qualifying for the race was a thrill for him. Dale Jr. finished 13th, and his father came in 21st. It was the first time that Dale Jr. had beaten his father in a Winston Cup race. Although Dale Sr. grumbled about following his son across the finish line, he was proud of him.

In his rookie season, Dale Jr. won his first Winston Cup race, the DIRECTV 500 at Texas Motor Speedway, in April. His father met him in the winner's circle. "I love you," Dale Sr. told his son, as Dale Jr. recalled in *Driver #8*. "I

This photo shows Dale Sr. (#3 Goodwrench black Chevrolet) and Dale Jr. (#8 Budweiser red Chevrolet) during a lap in the NASCAR Winston Cup Daytona 500 on February 18, 2001.

want to make sure you take the time to enjoy this and enjoy what you accomplished today." Dale Jr.'s success seemed to bring new energy to his father's racing career. That year, Dale Sr. finished second in the Winston Cup standings.

In October 2000, Dale Jr. wrote a loving tribute to his father and posted it on the NASCAR Web site. It is titled "I Know a Man." He wrote, "This man could lead the world's finest army. He has wisdom that knows no bounds. No fire could burn his character, no stone could break it . . . he stands as an example of what hard work and dedication will achieve." When his father

Emergency vehicles arrive at the wreckage from the crash that killed Dale Sr. at the 43rd Daytona 500 on February 18, 2001. Dale Sr.'s #3 black Chevrolet was bumped into a spin near turn 4 in the final lap of the race.

read it, Dale Jr. recalled in *Driver #8*, "he gave me a hug and told me how much he liked it and I thought for a second we were both gonna cry, which doesn't happen at all with the Earnhardt men."

COMING BACK AFTER TRAGEDY

The last thing Dale Jr. remembers his father saying to him on February 18, 2001, was that his car was good enough to win the Daytona 500. Dale Sr. predicted that the first, second, and third spots in the race were going to go to Dale Jr., himself, and Michael Waltrip.

Dale Sr.'s prediction was very close to being right. But then, on the last turn of the last lap of the Daytona 500, tragedy struck. The world lost a driving legend. Dale Jr. lost his father.

The first few days after his father's death were "the emptiest days of my life," Dale Jr. wrote in *Driver #8*. Although he was surrounded by fans and members of the media, he felt totally alone.

To help heal from his loss, Dale Jr. decided to start racing again just one week after his father's death because he truly loved the sport. Some people said it was too soon, but Dale Jr. defended his decision. "It's what my father would have done. It's

Dale Jr. celebrates after winning the Daytona 500 on February 15, 2004. He beat Tony Stewart by 0.273 seconds.

what he would have wanted me to do," he told *Scholastic Action* in 2002.

The race was at Rockingham Speedway in North Carolina. Just a few minutes after the crowd had observed a moment of silence in memory of his father and the race had begun, Dale Jr. crashed his car into the wall on the very first lap. The fans were stunned, but he walked away from the accident unhurt.

In July 2001, Dale Jr. returned to Daytona International Speedway for the Pepsi 400. It was the first time he had been to that track since his father's death. Before the race, he visited the turn where his father had died. The skid marks from the crash could still be seen on the pavement.

Although the first lap was hard for Dale Jr., it got easier as he started focusing more on the race. Michael Waltrip stayed close behind him. With Michael's help, Dale Jr. won the race.

In 2004, it was Dale Jr.'s turn to shine at the Daytona 500. It was a very emotional moment for him. This was the race that had claimed his father's life just three years earlier. With less than 20 laps to go, Dale Jr. swerved around driver Tony Stewart in a maneuver that Dale Sr. himself might have made. After he crossed the finish line in first place, Dale Jr. pulled his car over, took off his helmet, and blew a kiss to the sky.

Chapter Four

THE EARNHARDT EMPIRE

As Dale Jr. mourned for his father, fans saw him as a connection to the hero they had lost. They would ask him to sign pictures and other memorabilia of his father. Before each race, NASCAR would hold ceremonies for Dale Earnhardt Sr., and much of the attention would focus on his son.

Dale Jr. was also starting to get attention for his own accomplishments on the track. By 2007, he had earned more than $46 million in winnings. He had also become NASCAR's most popular driver. Dale Jr. was asked to star in commercials for everything from car parts to razors. He even acted in a few television shows.

THE DEI EMPIRE

Several years after Dale Sr.'s death, his fans continue to hold on to his memory. Every day, tour buses arrive at the DEI headquarters in Mooresville to remember his legacy. Many fans still wear hats, T-shirts, and other merchandise with the #3 on them. They tour the museum, looking at Dale Sr.'s many cars and trophies. They buy jackets, calendars, posters, and other Dale Earnhardt merchandise in the DEI gift shop.

Many fans also visit Daytona International Speedway, the place where Dale Sr. drove his final race. At the entrance, they find a small, circular garden. In the center of the circle is a bronze statue of Dale Sr. standing on

Dale Jr. autographs memorabilia for fans at the NASCAR Sprint Cup Series qualifying race at Michigan International Speedway in Brooklyn, Michigan. His fans have stuck by him in good times and bad.

a pedestal of the #3. It is there to commemorate Dale Sr.'s 1998 victory at the Daytona 500—the race that took him 20 tries to win. The statue shows him holding the 1998 Daytona trophy in his right hand. His left arm is raised, with his hand clenched, in triumph.

CONTINUING THE TRADITION

Dale Earnhardt Sr. has left a long racing legacy, inspiring generations of fans and future drivers. He has also left behind a lasting commitment to important causes. The Dale Earnhardt Foundation continues to contribute to charities that benefit children, education, and the environment. In 2004, the foundation partnered with *American Forests* magazine to plant 77,000 trees in Charlotte, North Carolina, to restore those lost to storms, disease, and development. The sevens in the number of trees represent Dale Sr.'s seven Winston Cup wins. In 2006, the Dale Earnhardt Foundation, Feed the Children, and the Boys & Girls Clubs of America held a special "Back to School" tour around the country to encourage children to study hard and remain in school. Participants received new backpacks and school supplies, and the local Boys & Girls Clubs

DALE JR.'S STATS

Dale Earnhardt Jr. is on his way to becoming a legend, just like his father. The following are some of his successes over the years:

1998 Seven Busch Series wins, Busch Series title

1999 Six Busch Series wins, Busch Series title, $162,095 in earnings, moved up to Winston Cup Series

2000 Two wins, 4 top 10 finishes, $2,610,400 in earnings

2001 Three wins, 15 top 10 finishes, $5,384,630 in earnings

2002 Two wins, 16 top 10 finishes, $4,570,980 in earnings

2003 Two wins, 21 top 10 finishes, $4,923,500 in earnings

2004 Six wins, 21 top 10 finishes, Daytona 500 win, $7,201,380 in earnings

2005 One win, 13 top 10 finishes, $5,761,830 in earnings

2006 One win, 17 top 10 finishes, $5,466,100 in earnings

2007 Zero wins, 12 top 10 finishes, $5,221,970 in earnings

2008 One win, 16 top 10 finishes, $4,611,290 in earnings

2009 Zero wins, 5 top 10 finishes, $3,417,964 (as of October 4)

(**Sources:** Dalejr.com and NASCAR.com)

received donations of books, video games, and stuffed toys for use in the local clubs. In addition, the Dale Earnhardt Foundation presents the Legend Leadership Award for candidates of any age who identify a problem or need in their community and have found a solution for that problem or need. Each winner receives a monetary grant for educational assistance and a trophy.

Dale Jr. continues to make his own mark as well. He's been chosen as NASCAR's most popular driver five times. He has also been listed as one of

Standing by her late husband's statue at Daytona International Speedway, Teresa Earnhardt holds a check for the Earnhardt Foundation. The foundation carries on Dale Sr.'s commitment to children, education, and the environment.

America's top 10 favorite athletes, alongside basketball legend Michael Jordan and golfer Tiger Woods, in an annual poll by Harris Interactive.

Dale Jr. is a successful businessman, too. He co-owns the racing team JR Motorsports, which has more than 100 employees. He is part owner of a racetrack in Kentucky and a motorsports complex near Mobile, Alabama.

Despite his many accomplishments, Dale Jr. still feels as though he lives in his father's shadow. That may be because he shares his father's aggressive driving style (although he makes contact with far fewer fenders on the track) and desire to win. Sometimes, the media and fans can't help but compare the two men.

Dale Jr. insists that he wants to be known not just because he is the son of Dale Earnhardt, but for his own successes as well. "The biggest compliment you can give me is that I remind you of my dad," he told *People* magazine in 2004. "But when is the day going to come when I don't have to reflect back? When will I stand on my own merit?"

The other question that remains is, "Will Dale Jr. be the last of the Earnhardt racing dynasty?" Not if he has anything to do with it. In 2004, he told *Men's Health* magazine that if he has a son one day, he would want him to race, too. Who knows? There might be another Earnhardt legend in the future.

1951

Dale Earnhardt Sr. is born on April 29 in Kannapolis, North Carolina.

1974

Dale Earnhardt Jr. is born on October 10 in Concord, North Carolina.

1975

Dale Sr. makes his stock car racing debut in the World 600 at Lowe's Motor Speedway in Charlotte, North Carolina.

1979

Dale Sr. wins his first race at Bristol Motor Speedway in Tennessee. He is also named Rookie of the Year.

1987

Dale Sr. makes his now-famous "Pass in the Grass."

1998

Dale Sr. wins the Daytona 500 on his 20th attempt. Dale Jr. wins the Busch Series title.

2000

Dale Sr., Dale Jr., and Kerry Earnhardt race together for the first and only time at the Pepsi 400 at Michigan International Speedway.

2001

Dale Sr. is killed in a crash on the last lap of the Daytona 500.

2003

Dale Jr. is named NASCAR's Most Popular Driver.

2004

Dale Jr. wins the Daytona 500.

2008

Dale Jr. wins the Chex Most Popular Driver Award for the sixth time. Dale Jr.'s team receives a Pit Road Award.

2009

Dale Jr. finishes 10th in the NASCAR Sprint All-Star Race in May.

accelerator The pedal that, when pressed with the foot, causes a car to speed up.

aggressive Bold, energetic, or forceful.

all-terrain vehicle (ATV) A compact motor vehicle with three or four wheels or treads that is designed to travel on all types of terrain, including roads.

asphalt The pavement on which cars are driven.

bumper cars An amusement park ride in which small electric cars with thick bumpers are driven into other such cars in an enclosed area.

cinderblock A lightweight building brick made from small cinders mixed with sand and cement.

go-kart A small four-wheeled vehicle with a lightweight or skeleton body that is used for racing.

grandstand The area where the audience sits to watch an auto race.

infield The area inside the racetrack.

Intimidator Dale Sr.'s nickname; someone who makes others afraid.

legacy Something that is passed down and treasured by the next generation.

memorabilia Souvenirs (for example, T-shirts or hats) that commemorate the history of a person or place.

National Association for Stock Car Auto Racing (NASCAR) The governing body for the sport of stock car racing.

pit An area of the racetrack where cars are refueled and repaired.

pit crew A race car driver's crew, which helps change tires and make repairs on the car during races.

prediction The act of forecasting something.

speedway A track for racing automobiles.

Sprint Cup Series Formerly called the Winston Cup, this is the top racing series in NASCAR.

stock car A racing car that is based on the same basic design as a car available for sale to the public.

tribute An acknowledgment of a respected person's contributions; to honor someone for his or her accomplishments.

Dale Earnhardt Foundation

1675 Dale Earnhardt Highway #3

Mooresville, NC 28115

(877) 334-DALE (3253)

Web site: http://www.daleearnhardtinc.com/Foundation

The mission of the Dale Earnhardt Foundation is to support charities that benefit children, education, and the environment.

Dale Earnhardt Jr. Foundation

P.O. Box 330

Mooresville, NC 28115

Web site: http://www.thedalejrfoundation.org

The Dale Earnhardt Jr. Foundation helps children achieve their dreams.

Daytona International Speedway

1801 West International Speedway Boulevard

Daytona Beach, FL 32114

(386) 254-2700

Web site: http://www.daytonainterntionalspeedway.com

Daytona International Speedway is the home of NASCAR's most important race, the Daytona 500, which is held annually in February.

NASCAR

P.O. Box 2875

Daytona Beach, FL 32120

(386) 253-0611

Web site: http://www.nascar.com

The National Association for Stock Car Racing, Inc., has been the governing body for stock car racing for 60 years. NASCAR is the number-one spectator sport in the world.

NASCAR Foundation

Two Wachovia Center

301 South Tryon Street, Suite 1710

Charlotte, NC 28202

(704) 348-9630

Web site: http://foundation.nascar.com

The NASCAR Foundation supports a number of charities. Many of these charities help children who are sick or poor.

National Auto Sport Association

P.O. Box 21555

Richmond, CA 94820

(510) 232-NASA (6272)

Web site: http://www.nasaproracing.com/aboutnasa/regions.html

The National Auto Sport Association has been in existence since 1991. Its goal is to promote the sport of auto racing to both professional racers and enthusiasts.

WEB SITES

Due to the changing nature of Internet links, Rosen Publishing has developed an online list of Web sites related to the subject of this book. This site is updated regularly. Please use this link to access the list:

http://www.rosenlinks.com/sfam/earn

FOR FURTHER READING

Armentrout, David, and Patricia Armentrout. *Dale Earnhardt Jr.* Vero Beach, FL: Rourke Publishers, 2004.

Barber, Phil. *Dale Earnhardt: The Likable Intimidator*. Excelsior, MN: Tradition Books, 2003.

Caldwell, Dave. *Speed Show: How NASCAR Won the Heart of America (A New York Times* Book). Boston, MA: Kingfisher, 2006.

Doeden, Matt. *Dale Earnhardt Jr.* (Sports Heroes and Legends). Minneapolis, MN: Lerner Publishing, 2005.

Gigliotti, Jim. *Dale Earnhardt Jr.* (The World of NASCAR). Mankato, MN: The Child's World, 2008.

Gigliotti, Jim. *Dale Earnhardt Jr.: Tragedy and Triumph*. Maple Plain, MN: Tradition Books, 2004.

Gillispie, Tom. *Angel in Black: Remembering Dale Earnhardt Sr.* Nashville, TN: Cumberland House Publishing, 2008.

Levy, Janey. *Dale Earnhardt Jr.* (Stock Car Racing). New York, NY: Children's Press, 2007.

NASCAR Scene Editors. *Thunder and Glory: The 25 Most Memorable Races in NASCAR Winston Cup History*. Chicago, IL: Triumph Books, 2006.

Roza, Greg. *Dale Earnhardt Jr.* (Behind the Wheel). New York, NY: Rosen Publishing, 2007.

Savage, Jeff. *Dale Earnhardt Jr.* Minneapolis, MN: Lerner Publications Company, 2006.

Schaefer, A. R. *Dale Earnhardt*. Mankato, MN: Capstone Press, 2007.

Stewart, Mark, and Mike Kennedy. *NASCAR Behind the Scenes* (The Science of NASCAR). Minneapolis, MN: Lerner Publications, 2007.

Woods, Bob. *Pit Pass: Behind the Scenes of NASCAR* (NASCAR Middle Grade Book). Pleasantville, NY: Reader's Digest Children's Books, 2005.

Anderson, Lars. "Here Comes Junior." *Sports Illustrated*, Vol. 101, Issue 14, October 11, 2004, pp. 64–65.

Anderson, Lars. "Junior Wins One for Dad." *Sports Illustrated*, Vol. 100, Issue 8, February 23, 2004, pp. 48–51.

Anderson, Lars. "Shootin' the Breeze with Junior." *Sports Illustrated*, Vol. 106, Issue 8, February 19, 2007, p. 89.

Anonymous. "A Career in Pictures Fast Track." *Sports Illustrated Presents Dale Earnhardt 1951–2001: A Tribute to the Man in Black, Special Commemorative Issue*, February 28, 2001, pp. 18–39.

Bechtel, Mark. "The Last Race." *Sports Illustrated Presents Dale Earnhardt 1951–2001: A Tribute to the Man in Black, Special Commemorative Issue*, February 28, 2001, pp. 62–71.

Bechtel, Mark, and Pete McEntegart. "Crushing." *Sports Illustrated. Death of a Champion: Dale Earnhardt 1951–2001*, Vol. 94, Issue 9, February 26, 2001, pp. 36–43.

Clattenburg, Will. "Planting Earnhardt's Forest." *American Forests*, Vol. 110, Summer 2004, pp. 26–31.

Deitsch, Richard, and Trisha Blackmar. "Remembering Dale." *Sports Illustrated Presents Dale Earnhardt 1951–2001: A Tribute to the Man in Black, Special Commemorative Issue*, February 28, 2001, pp. 74–79.

Earnhardt, Dale, Jr. *Driver #8*. New York, NY: Warner Books, Inc., 2002.

Earnhardt, Dale, Jr. "My Biography." Retrieved January 25, 2009 (http://www.dalejr.com/#aboutme/bio).

Hastings, Michael. "Dale Earnhardt Jr." *Scholastic Action*, Vol. 25, Issue 12, March 25, 2002, pp. 6–7.

Hewitt, Bill. "A Hero's Last Lap." *People*, Vol. 55, Issue 9, March 5, 2001, pp. 100–105.

Lambert, Pam. "Junior Achievement. *People*, Vol. 61, Issue 9, March 8, 2004, pp. 71–72.

Lambert, Pam, Johnny Dodd, Michaele Ballard, and Andrea Billups. "Sudden Impact." *People*, Vol. 62, Issue 5, August 2, 2004, pp. 62–64.

McCrumb, Sharyn. *St. Dale*. New York, NY: Kensington Books, 2005.

Montville, Leigh. *At the Altar of Speed: The Fast Life and Tragic Death of Dale Earnhardt*. New York, NY: Random House, 2001.

NASCAR.com. "Angels to Feature Girl Who Gave Earnhardt 500 Penny." February 26, 2009. Retrieved April 4, 2009 (http://www.nascar.com/2009/news/headlines/official/02/26/wessa.miller.penny.dearnhardt/index.html).

Quill, Scott. "Driving Force." *Men's Health*, Vol. 19, Issue 4, May 2004, pp. 96–97.

Savage, Jeff. *Dale Earnhardt Jr.* Minneapolis, MN: Lerner Publications Company, 2006.

Schaefer, A. R. *Dale Earnhardt*. Mankato, MN: Capstone Press, 2007.

SportingNews.com. "Earnhardt Killed in Last-Lap Crash at Daytona." February 18, 2001. Retrieved January 25, 2009 (http://www.sportingnews.com/archives/Earnhardt/sadday/html).

SportingNews.com. "Earnhardt Timeline." Retrieved January 25, 2009 (http://www.sportingnews.com/archives/Earnhardt/timeline.html).

Sullivan, Robert. "The Last Lap—Dale Earnhardt: 1951–2001." *Time*, Vol. 157, Issue 9, March 5, 2001, pp. 60–69.

INDEX

ABOUT THE AUTHOR

Stephanie Watson is an award-winning writer who is based in Atlanta, Georgia. She is a regular contributor to several online and print publications, and she has written or contributed to more than two dozen books, including *Anderson Cooper: Profile of a TV Journalist*, *Celebrity Biographies: Daniel Radcliffe*, and *Weird, Wacky and Wild Georgia Trivia*. She has also written articles for HowStuffWorks.com.

PHOTO CREDITS

Designer: Les Kanturek; Editor: Kathy Kuhtz Campbell; Photo Researcher: Marty Levick